BY MJ KEATTS

D1235852

Conducting

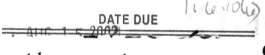

gs

A guide to running
productive community
association board
meetings

COMMUNITY
ASSOCIATIONS
INSTITUTE

225 Reinekers Lane, Suite 300
Alexandria, VA 22314
(703) 548-8600

Community Associations Institute
225 Reinekers Lane, Suite 300
Alexandria, VA 22314

The Community Associations Institute is a national, nonprofit organization
created in 1973 to educate and represent America's residential community association industry. It is a multidisciplinary alliance leading the industry and foster-
ing effective community associations.

*This publication is designed to provide accurate and authoritative information in regard to the
subject matter covered. It is sold with the understanding that the publisher is not engaged in
rendering legal, accounting, or other professional service. If legal advice or other expert assistance is required, the services of a competent professional person should be sought.*

—From a Declaration of Principles jointly adopted by a committee of the American Bar
Association and a Committee of Publishers.

Library of Congress Cataloging-in-Publication Data

Conducting Meetings: A guide to running productive community association board
    meetings / edited by MJ Keatts.
        p.   cm.
    Includes bibliographical references and index.
    ISBN 0-941301-42-7
    1. Condominium associations—United States—Management.
2. Homeowners' associations—United States—Management. 3. Housing management—United States.   I. Keatts, MJ (Marci Joh), 1971—
HD7287.67.U5C653   1998
643'.2—dc21
                                                        98-11307
                                                        CIP

CONTENTS

INTRODUCTION

IT'S THE MONTHLY BOARD MEETING, and you're meeting in the kitchen of the president's home. The first item on the agenda? Chaos. As the secretary reviews the minutes, Little Jimmy, the president's three-year-old son, bangs a drum and parades around the table. Older son Joey fights with his sister over the television, which is only slightly louder than an Apollo moon launch. Freida, the treasurer, continually leaves the table to grab doughnuts, while Fred, a homeowner whose voice is actually louder than the TV, lobbies for approval of his Brady Bunch garden gnomes. With each interruption, the discussion strays to new and unrelated topics—when Freida explains the relationship between pet problems and UFO abductions, the president searches for the agenda, which, unfortunately, was eaten by the dog. Finally, after four hours and 16 minutes, the meeting adjourns, due to a lack of additional doughnuts.

This is not the way to hold a board meeting.

A board meeting is not a social meeting. It's not a time to gossip, to socialize, or to promote a personal agenda. It's a business meeting. And if your board meetings are lasting longer than two hours—with nothing accomplished—then something is wrong. Maybe it's the environment. Maybe it's disorganization. Maybe it's a lack of leadership.

Unproductive meetings create unproductive boards. They increase frustration, destroy morale, and make it harder to recruit volunteers. They also waste everyone's time.

This book, a compilation of previously published *Common Ground* and *Community Management* articles, helps community association directors and managers run effective, efficient board meetings. It also discusses how to prepare for a meeting, how to take proper meeting minutes, the potential benefits and drawbacks of recording meetings, and appropriate agenda items for executive sessions.

Productive board meetings are the foundation of a successful community association. They are meetings that follow a detailed agenda. They are meetings that avoid irrelevant side topics. They are meetings that result in decisions.

No one wants to waste their valuable time in a long, combative, unproductive meeting. By following the steps in this book, directors and managers can conduct productive meetings—in less than two hours—that improve the association's reputation and its effectiveness.

CHAPTER 1

Proper Meeting Preparation

by Pam Washburn, CMCA, AMS

Board Packets Help Reduce Meeting Times

ARE BOARD MEMBERS
READY TO TAKE
ACTION?

DO YOUR BOARD MEETINGS last for hours? If so, it could be because your board members aren't prepared. And if they're not prepared, they're probably not receiving a board packet (or they're receiving a packet so unorganized that it's impossible to comprehend).

Managers should prepare and distribute board packets 10 days before each board meeting. The packet should include minutes from the previous meeting; finance, committee, management, and treasurer's reports; correspondence; and, most importantly, the meeting agenda. Preparing the packet will take time, but it will ultimately save time. It will lead to better informed, better prepared boards, and smoother, more efficient meetings.

Effective Agendas

An effective agenda is the backbone of the board packet. The agenda should include enough details to help board members prepare for the meeting. Simply stating "Treasurer's Report" or "New Business" is not enough. Under each agenda heading, list the main points that will be discussed. An example might be:

NEW BUSINESS: (10:50 a.m.)
- A. Recommendation to approve Exterior Change Request No. 8279 to install plantings on the common grounds at the rear of the lot line.
- B. Recommendations from the Safety and Security Committee to make improvements to the entrance security systems.
- C. Discussion on issues regarding upcoming budget preparation.
  - ✦ Board's opinions regarding user fee increases.

- Board's priorities for capital acquisitions.
- Management's projections regarding annual costs to operate new Pitch and Putt golf course.

Also include benchmark times on the agenda. For example, "Call to Order—10:00 a.m.," "Approval of Minutes—10:05." This lets board members know how time will be allotted and keeps the meeting moving. At my association, we typically schedule two-hour board meetings. The agendas also include the times and dates of future board meetings, workshops, and events, to further allow directors to plan.

Organizing the Packet

The meeting packet should be prepared in the same chronological order as the agenda. Use colored paper or tabs to mark the beginning of different sections. Label each item to correspond with the agenda. You can also design a form to serve as the cover sheet for each packet item. The form should contain brief background facts, committee recommendations if applicable, and management's recommendations.

If you do not use a form, be sure to include your recommendations on key agenda items with your monthly manager's report. Board meetings are not the place to tell directors how you feel. Prepare them ahead of time.

The packet material should be concise and complete. I find it helpful to prepare the agenda throughout the month, and make copies of the packet items as time permits. However you do it, board packets work. They enable your board members to arrive at meetings prepared to take action. The board of directors at my association consistently completes the agenda—without spending hours in the meeting. ❧

Pam Washburn, CMCA, AMS, is vice president of operations for the Timber Pines Community Association, Inc. in Spring Hill, Florida.

by Kenneth Budd
and MJ Keatts

Advance Planning Boosts
Board Productivity

STUDY SESSIONS AND
ADVANCE INFORMATION
HELP DIRECTORS PREPARE

MEETINGS AT SHELTER CREEK, a 1,296-unit community in San Bruno, California, used to last three to four hours. Now they last no more than two hours. Mike Yarman, CMCA, AMS, Shelter Creek's manager, attributes the improvement to advance planning. He meets with the president the night before the meeting to discuss the agenda. If the agenda is particularly full, he holds a 45-minute study session two weeks before the meeting.

The study session is an open forum for directors and members. For example, if the association was scheduled to decide on an insurance contract at its next meeting, insurance representatives would be invited to the study session to answer questions.

Rob Felix, CMCA, PCAM, manager of the Sun City Vistoso Community Association in Tucson, Arizona, agrees that advance planning helps directors prepare for board meetings. Felix distributes information packets to each board member one week before the meeting. The packets include copies of the meeting agenda, treasurer's report, committee reports, management report, minutes from the last board meeting and any pertinent correspondence or documents. By giving board members a chance to review the agenda before the meeting, Felix can answer their questions and is able to anticipate potential problems.

Felix also discusses the agenda with the president before the meeting and offers advice on the issues at hand. After he meets with the president, he knows if he needs to collect more information.

Bill Overton, PCAM, manager of the Wailea Community Association in Maui, Hawaii, also distributes information packets to board members before the meeting. In addition to discussing the agenda with the president, he summarizes the association's business and his recommendations in a cover letter, which he inserts in the front of board members' information packets.

"I use the cover letter to present my recommendations to the board in writing," Overton said. "Sometimes board members respond better to a recommendation when it's presented in writing than when it's presented orally. If a manager seems pushy in a meeting, the board reacts negatively."

Managers will know they have adequately prepared for a meeting when board members aren't peppering them with questions. "The board will be ready to govern and won't require any additional information," Overton said.

"Preparing for a board meeting is like preparing for court," said Linnea Juarez, PCAM, president of Condominium Financial Management, Inc. in Martinez, California. "Managers must have their arguments laid out and anticipate [board members'] cross examination."

Juarez, who teaches managers how to effectively organize and facilitate board meetings, once observed a board meeting where the manager presented three bids for a fence that needed repair. "Didn't we have this fence fixed two years ago?" a board member asked the manager. "Who fixed it then?" The manager did not know.

"The manager should have collected this information when he was preparing for the meeting," Juarez said. "He didn't do his homework."

Strict Agendas Maintain Structure

Regardless of how well a manager prepares for a meeting, there is always the chance that a rambling speaker could jeopardize the board's productivity. Agendas with time limits, however, enable the president to effectively guide meeting discussions.

Joseph Carleton, Jr., a Maine attorney and legislator who is writing a book on meetings, says an agenda with start times and time limits gives a board meeting structure.

"They make directors more aware of time," Carleton said.

"They provide a subtle reminder if you're falling behind in the discussion." Carleton also suggests that the president remind directors of time limits before the meeting begins.

When a board is expecting a large, demanding audience—perhaps due to a large special assessment or an unattended maintenance problem—it may consider beginning its agenda by allowing 20-30 minutes for comments from the crowd. If owners are still asking questions after 30 minutes, the board president should announce that he or she will take three more questions. This strategy lets owners know that their time is up, but keeps them from feeling cut off by the president. ❧

Kenneth Budd is CAI's director of publications and editor of Common Ground. *MJ Keatts is editor of* Community Management.

by Kenneth Budd

Boards Can't Conduct Business in the Kitchen

FINDING A SUITABLE LOCATION AND TIME FOR BOARD MEETINGS

WHEN BOARD MEMBERS began bringing food scraps to meetings, Judy Burd, CMCA, AMS, PCAM, knew there was a problem. Actually, there were two problems: two fluffy little dogs named Yip and Yap, as Burd, of Legum & Norman, Inc. in McLean, Virginia, liked to call them.

Yip and Yap belonged to a board member who brought them to every meeting. The dogs would scamper about the room, yipping and yapping. Directors brought food scraps to keep the dogs quiet. At the end of the director's term, she moved to a neighboring building. Her reputation preceded her. When Yip and Yap moved in, the board of directors passed a rule stating that "no pets are permitted to attend meetings of the association."

Eliminating distractions is essential for running a meeting. Would IBM hold an important board meeting with dogs scurrying around the room? Hopefully not.

IBM also wouldn't hold a meeting in the CEO's kitchen. Meetings should be held in an environment that enhances productivity. A meeting in a board member's home will typically invite more distractions, from pets to the television. Consider more formal settings—if the association has a clubhouse, find an available room. If the manager has an office, hold the meeting there. Many public libraries have meeting rooms available for minimal fees.

"It helps maintain a business-like atmosphere," said Joseph Carleton, Jr., a Maine attorney and legislator.

Some meeting experts believe a business-like setting does not include food. Food can be disruptive—imagine directors munching on corn chips during the management report. According to Carleton, refreshments are fine for the beginning of the meeting, or at a break in the middle, but not during the meeting. That said, some associations serve cookies, sodas, and coffee during their meetings because they feel it creates a nicer atmosphere.

One thing that does not create a nicer atmosphere, Burd said, are cigarettes. She believes cigarettes are distracting—her board meetings are strictly nonsmoking. Alcohol is even worse. It affects decision making—and an empty wine bottle usually corresponds with diminished productivity.

"I don't like the connotations of having alcohol at a meeting," Burd said. "If there is a controversial decision, or if a director seems out of control, residents could later say the director was drunk."

Day Break or Nightfall

When is the best time of day to hold meetings? It depends on board members' personalities and time constraints. What works for one board may not work for another.

There are pros and cons for various times. David Gibbons,

Encouraging Board Members to Show

Directors who perpetually arrive late to meetings—or who don't show at all—can stifle a board's productivity. Here are some common reasons for board member tardiness and absenteeism and some ways to prevent such habits from jeopardizing board effectiveness.

Reasons for Tardiness
- Most board members juggle family, business and community responsibilities

- Some associations hold board meetings too frequently

- Meetings exceed two hours and are perceived as unproductive

- Association bylaws lack clearly defined board member roles and responsibilities

- Association bylaws lack penalties for failure to attend board meetings

- Some boards provide insufficient notice of schedule changes

Possible Solutions
- Explain the importance of attending meetings to current and incoming board members; ask frequent absentees if they really want to continue serving on the board

- Amend association bylaws to mandate dismissal from the board after two consecutive unexcused absences

- Survey members at each meeting—and follow-up with absent members—to learn the best time for the next meeting

- Institute a buddy system to keep members informed when they miss a meeting

Source: Development and Technical Assistance Center in New Haven, Connecticut

CMCA, PCAM, CPM, of Quadrant, Inc. in Myrtle Beach, South Carolina and a former CAI president, is a proponent of day meetings. Gibbons believes directors need to be at their top mental and physical condition when meeting. That is difficult after working an eight-hour day, fighting rush-hour traffic, and wolfing down a quick meal and a cocktail (or after no meal at all). Gibbons thinks directors should meet early, at 7:00 or 7:30 a.m., before heading to work. This inspires them to hold quicker, more efficient meetings. Another alternative is to hold the meeting at 4:00 or 4:30 in the afternoon, rather than late in the evening.

Others argue that day meetings are unrealistic and more likely to exclude homeowners who work. So what's the best evening time? Mike Yarman, CMCA, AMS, has found that the last Wednesday of the month at 7:00 p.m. works best for both board members and homeowners at Shelter Creek in San Bruno, California. Rather than stressing out directors, Yarman thinks the 7:00 p.m. start time gives them time to get home from work, unwind, and have dinner before attending the meeting. Others suggest 7:30 p.m.

While there is no consensus on when to hold a meeting, most experts agree that meetings should not last more than two hours.

"Most people become unproductive after an hour-and-a half," Carleton said. "At that point, it may be more productive to continue at another time." As Gibbons noted, when tired, frustrated people make rash, last-second decisions, the result can be an even longer meeting filled with hundreds of angry owners.

As community manager Stephen Margolis wrote in a 1997 *Common Ground* article, boards also should examine the frequency of their meetings. Some boards believe meetings must be held monthly. This is not true. Unless the association documents or state statutes dictate meeting times, meetings may be called when needed. Most associations can be just as effective with less than one meeting a month. If a meeting is run efficiently and effectively, board members will be happier—and they will need to schedule fewer meetings. ❧

Kenneth Budd is CAI's director of publications and editor of Common Ground.

CHAPTER 2

Staying on Course

by Kenneth Budd

Keeping the Meeting Moving

DON'T LET RAMBLING DISCUSSIONS IMPEDE PROGRESS

WRITING AN AGENDA and preparing board packets does not guarantee an effective meeting. Boards of directors often stray from the agenda, which adds countless minutes to the meeting—a discussion on pool contracts leads to a discussion on pool halls, which results in a 15-minute debate on *The Music Man*. Keeping the discussion focused on association business is the responsibility of the meeting chair—typically, the president.

"The president determines the flow of business," said Joseph Carleton, Jr., a Maine attorney and legislator. "He or she keeps the others in check and suggests when it's time to stop talking and start voting." The president, Carleton said, is the mediator—the guiding force who prevents 30-minute monologues and gossip sessions, and searches for consensus in the group. When the discussion deteriorates or heads in another direction, the president needs to steer it back. The manager also can help keep the meeting on track.

As part of the steering process, Florida manager Brent Herrington, PCAM, has another suggestion: never present an issue—particularly a minor one—without a proposed solution.

"Any time you dangle a topic in front of a group of people and invite them to opine about it, everyone will feel challenged to weigh-in with some insightful observations and off-the-cuff opinions," said Herrington, in a message posted on CAI's web site. Instead, Herrington recommends that the manager, the president, or a committee research issues before the meeting and propose solutions.

For example, if a resident inquires about extending the pool hours, the president or manager can say: "For the next item on the agenda, I recommend we revise our pool rules so the facility can remain open until 10:00 p.m. during the months of June, July, and August. This is in response to a member request. I have weighed the pros and cons and believe it will be a positive change for the community. Assuming the board is supportive, I would like to announce this change in the May newsletter, with the condition that the change is on a trial basis and will be reevaluated in July. Is there a motion to approve my recommendation?"

You may have just saved 30 minutes.

As the manual for CAI's M-100 course explains, meetings are for making decisions. A board meeting is not the time to begin the decision-making process or discuss minor issues.

"The board shouldn't have to discuss late fees—the manager should handle that," said Linda Farsi, CMCA, PCAM, vice president of Community Group in Virginia Beach, Virginia. Farsi wrote about meetings for CAI's Southeastern Virginia Chapter. "Meetings shouldn't be an occasion to micromanage the manager. The board should be making decisions about important issues, like contracts and large expenditures."

Diffusing Meeting Conflicts

Conflicts often come to a head in board meetings, particularly when directors feel shut out of the decision-making process. Excluded from the debate, that person sits and stews, brewing with hostility. How can you prevent that anger from building? By giving each director a chance to contribute.

Sam Dolnick, former president of the Lake Park Condominium Association in La Mesa, California, and a former member of CAI's Board of Trustees, said his association posts its agendas 14 days before a meeting. Members of the board can add or remove topics within seven days, at which point the final agenda is posted. At the meeting, the president will ask if an emergency has arisen that should be added to the agenda. This gives everyone at least two opportunities to add agenda items.

But this is only the first step. Once the meeting starts, each di-

Television Camera Helps Restore Meeting Order

By MJ Keatts

Before Canyon Lakes Property Association began televising board meetings in the mid-1980s, dissension among members sometimes turned into violent quarrels.

Rolling the camera helped Canyon Lakes retain meeting order, but not without a few drawbacks.

While out-of-control board meetings are a thing of the past for the California association, so are large homeowner turnouts. Unless a hot item, such as an assessment increase, is on the agenda, about 10 of the association's 13,000 residents usually attend each board meeting.

"A good number of the residents watch the meetings on television," said former manager Bill Hallman, CMCA, PCAM. "Some residents show up at the end of the meeting to make a statement."

Residents who watch the meeting on television, but do not attend the premeeting work session, only see the second half of the show.

Because board members discuss the agenda items during the premeeting work session, which is not televised, they usually do not debate during the board meeting. Only homeowners who attend the work session will know board members' positions on the agenda items.

"Being on television limits board members' ability to really discuss the issues," Hallman said. "When there are two cameras in the room, you're very aware of what you're saying."

rector—not one dominant personality—needs time to express his or her views.

"One of the best ways to defuse a potentially volatile situation is to give a person time to talk," said Ellen Hirsch de Haan, an attorney with Becker & Poliakoff in St. Petersburg, Florida and a member of CAI's Executive Committee. "Courtesy can make a difference."

Courtesy also means that everyone speaks for the same amount of time. Boards may want to write regulations for this— for example, each person can speak for three minutes, and can't speak again until everyone has spoken. Such a procedure ensures fairness and prevents frustration from building in less vocal directors. Otherwise, Dolnick said, some people will speak more than others, and the president could be accused of favoritism.

Equal time, however, should be matched by equal protection—specifically protection from personal attacks.

"When anyone makes a personal attack, the gavel goes down," Dolnick said. "That's out of order. Name calling and interrupting are destructive."

Finally, if meetings are constantly plagued by "demagogue" owners determined to "divide and conquer" board unity, consider asking an off-duty, uniformed police officer to observe the meeting. Though the officer will have no power at the meeting, most attendees will respond with respect.

Parliamentary Procedure

A structured meeting—one that follows *Robert's Rules of Order* or some form of parliamentary procedure—also can help control conflicts. Parliamentary procedure is a set of rules for conducting meetings. The most popular version of parliamentary procedure is *Robert's Rules of Order*.

Parliamentary procedures should be consistent. Directors should not cite obscure technicalities from *Robert's Rules* if the board does not normally use them. That in itself will create conflict, not control. Sam Gladding, a professor at Wake Forest University who specializes in counseling and group work, believes boards should not feel compelled to use *Robert's Rules* if it is causing frustration.

"It's not the only way to run a group," Gladding said. "*Robert's Rules* tend to make a group more stiff and formal. Many times it inhibits real conversation rather than facilitating it." Organized discussion, Gladding believes, is the critical component in making decisions—and casting votes—that don't destroy a group. Voting can create winners and losers. For the losers, Gladding said, the result can be either great apathy or great hostility. Forcing a decision down others' throats and not building some form of consensus is a recipe for conflict. According to Robert Dennistoun, author of CAI's *GAP 23—The Role of the Association President*, ideas need to be explained, not proclaimed.

"If the goal is to advance an idea and to convince people of it, you need to do your homework and discuss it," Dennistoun said. "Votes don't change things—they validate them. It's the discussion that matters." ❧

Kenneth Budd is CAI's director of publications and editor of Common Ground.

by Harold Corbin

Parliamentarians Offer Guidance on Meeting Procedures

HIRING AN EXPERT TO HELP MAINTAIN ORDER

AN ASSOCIATION BOARD MEETING is the place for members to resolve old business and discuss new plans. But unless meetings are run in a well-organized manner, chaos can, and frequently does, reign. To ensure that everyone has a fair hearing, that members' rights are protected, and that the meeting's objectives are met, the association needs to follow parliamentary procedure.

Some associations have members who are well-versed in the intricacies of parliamentary procedure. But other associations may need to employ a professional parliamentarian.

Whether volunteer or paid, the parliamentarian must be familiar with the association's bylaws, standing rules, and procedures, as well as the minutes of the last meeting. Additionally, the

Don't Be Afraid of Parliamentary Procedure

Parliamentary procedure is vital for a smooth-running meeting. But *Robert's Rules of Order*—the bible of parliamentary procedure—can be difficult to understand. Fortunately, there are some basic rules of parliamentary procedure that every association can easily follow. They include:

- Follow the agenda
- Discuss one subject at a time
- Give each board member a chance to speak
- Speak only on the issue being discussed
- Speak only when recognized by the chair
- Address questions and comments to the chair
- Decide issues through motions, seconds, and votes

parliamentarian must be familiar with the meeting agenda, ensure that it is followed, and that questions are handled appropriately.

It is not the parliamentarian's job to control the meeting, but rather to advise and maintain order. He may remain inactive, offering advice only when questioned directly, or become an active participant, speaking to the assembled members and explaining opinions.

An experienced parliamentarian's fee should be based on the amount of time he is expected to spend preparing for and attending the board meeting. Generally, the association also pays for the parliamentarian's travel expenses.

Hiring a parliamentarian to attend board meetings is a sound investment. A parliamentarian who is impartial, consistent, and tactful is invaluable not only to the presiding officer but to the entire association as well. ❧

Harold Corbin is a practitioner of parliamentary procedure and a long-time member of the American Institute of Parliamentarians.

by Peter Philbin

Swatting at Gadflies
HOW PARLIAMENTARY PROCEDURE CAN TAKE THE BITE OUT OF GADFLIES

THE MEETING IS GOING WELL, when suddenly there is a disturbing buzzing noise. Flying dangerously around the room is an angry, insect-like creature, and it is blaming the association for everything from an assessment increase to a noisy next-door neighbor. It is the dreaded gadfly.

The gadfly is an expert at criticizing, cajoling, and pinpointing the errors of others. It demands change, but rarely devotes the time or effort needed to create positive change. The gadfly may mean well, but it never channels those good intentions into constructive efforts.

The gadfly often emerges at association meetings and creates an atmosphere of chaos and paralysis. The gadfly raises parliamentary issues, alleges noncompliance with statutory or governing document provisions, and constantly interrupts. It attacks board members' personal integrity and alleges conflicts of interest.

Dissent can be healthy and productive and is an essential part of the democratic process. But gadflies and dissenters are two different creatures. Dissenters may disagree with an approach, but they offer alternatives and work within the established rules to accomplish their goals. Gadflies ignore rules of order, are rude, disregard the process, and only appear satisfied when their demands are met. Some associations create gadflies by not keeping their members informed. Some members, however, are born gadflies—and even one gadfly can infect a meeting with confusion. What can the board or manager do to maintain order?

It's Not a Homeowner Meeting
When dealing with a gadfly in a board meeting, remember that these are not homeowner meetings. The meeting is for the board to conduct the business of the association.

While community associations should open their meetings and

generally are required to by law, this does not mean that owners are entitled to interrupt meetings by speaking out of turn and raising irrelevant issues. There are several ways to deal with the gadfly in this setting:

Announce meeting procedures. Sometimes owners who attend board meetings are not familiar with meeting procedure. At the beginning of the meeting, the presiding officer should explain the meeting process and state when the board will accept comments from homeowners. If the presiding officer announces that the board will not allow homeowner comments, then it must follow this policy consistently—not just with the gadfly. It is sometimes difficult to enforce a policy limiting homeowner comments, especially when the vast majority of the meeting attendants are prepared to provide constructive suggestions or helpful information. But if the primary goal is to constrain the gadfly, then the board must enforce the restriction uniformly for it to be effective.

Host a homeowner forum. Many boards schedule a few minutes before or after the meeting for owners to express their thoughts. The time limit per person may depend on the number of owners at the meeting and the business at hand. Many associations allow each resident three-to-five minutes to speak. But at the end of the allotted time (a total of 20-30 minutes maximum), the board moves on to its planned agenda. Some boards will pass a rule of order requiring owners who wish to speak at the meeting to notify the board or manager in writing. Such a rule helps the board plan its agenda and discourages aimless or spontaneous homeowner speeches. Association documents and state statutes rarely require such a forum; however, it can be an effective way for the board and management to stay in touch with the community and maintain meeting control. A forum also gives the gadfly a chance to "vent" at one specified time—hopefully reducing the gadfly's tendency to interrupt throughout the meeting. It is best to hold the homeowner forum before or after the meeting. This way, the gadfly's statements are not part of the official record.

Don't respond with anger. The board and management must not argue or trade insults with the gadfly. Usually it is best to let

Can the Gadfly be Tamed?

By Kenneth Budd

Taming the gadfly is difficult, but not impossible. According to James Cachine, AMS, PCAM, of Legum & Norman, Inc. in McLean, Virginia, one trick is to assign the gadfly a special project or appoint it to a committee.

"This can give them a new perspective on the association and encourage them to work with you, instead of against you," said Cachine, a *Common Ground* contributing editor. "They begin to see things differently."

Another way to tame the gadfly is simply to call its bluff. Jerry Fien, a New Jersey homeowner and former CAI trustee, says that if a difficult resident begins to complain loudly enough, he'll ask, "What would you recommend?"

"They usually don't have an answer," Fien said.

Cachine adds that since most gadflies rarely want to become involved in the association, asking them to volunteer can be a way to frighten them off. "Once they see that you want them to do some work, they become less involved," he said.

the gadfly complain for a few minutes during the homeowner forum and then buzz away. Remember, the gadfly is energized by hostility or confrontation. If a response is necessary, the board or management can wait until after the homeowner forum and "correct" the record. The board does not need to engage the gadfly or give it rebuttal time.

Utilize parliamentary control. Parliamentary control means knowing when and how to (1) table a motion; (2) postpone a motion indefinitely; (3) refer a matter to a committee; (4) adopt special rules of order; and (5) limit debate.

Parliamentary authority was created to bring order to a proceeding. A good working knowledge of parliamentary authority can mean the difference between paralysis and efficiency. If the association's governing documents or state statutes do not specify such authority, the board should adopt a rule of order requiring the use of parliamentary procedure.

Gadflies on the Board

Controlling gadflies who serve on the board is a bit more complex than diffusing gadflies sitting in the audience. If a gadfly is serving on the board, the association could face political gridlock.

Gadfly board members may harp on pet issues or repeatedly demand the board to review a proposed action. An unprepared board or chairperson may improperly refuse to recognize motions or allow discussion on the matter. Other chairpersons will allow the gadfly to drone on until some type of motion is presented and defeated—after a lot of wasted time and energy.

To prevent this, the chairperson or president may need to plan a strategy with other members before the meeting. For example, by anticipating the gadfly's motion, the prepared members can move to postpone it indefinitely. If the motion to postpone indefinitely is adopted, the gadfly's motion is essentially dead unless revived by a motion to reconsider.

Sometimes the gadfly's actions become too disruptive and the board needs to propose the member's removal to the membership—before productive board members resign *en masse*. The board should carefully consider such a proposal, since members will certainly ask about it. Explanations, if any, must be clearly presented and supported by facts. Simply scheduling the meeting may prompt the gadfly to resign voluntarily.

Board meetings do not need to dissolve into paralysis. By understanding the purpose of the meeting, the rights and obligations of the parties, and parliamentary authority, boards can conduct the business of the association. ❧

Peter Philbin is an attorney with Rees, Broome & Diaz, P.C. in Vienna, Virginia.

CHAPTER 3

Taking
Meeting
Minutes

by Gurdon Buck

Make Meeting Minutes Matter | HOW TO TAKE PERFECTLY PROPER MINUTES

MEETING MINUTES are an association's only official record of its board, committee or membership decisions and actions. Therefore, it is imperative that these records are properly taken.

To begin with, the worst basis for a set of good minutes is a bad meeting. If the president or chair fails to follow parliamentary procedure or understand the fundamentals of running a meeting, the resulting minutes will reflect the inevitable chaos.

Meeting minutes reflect what the assembly decides, not what its members say. An assembly is the group of individuals at a board, committee or membership meeting responsible for making decisions. If a meeting goes by without a vote or official action being taken, it isn't a meeting, but rather a random gathering of people. Minutes of such a gathering should merely reflect the calling of the opening of the meeting and its adjournment.

An assembly should have rules of order. Either the rules of order should be included in the association bylaws, or the assembly can adopt the rules of order at the beginning of each meeting. *Robert's Rules of Order* serves as the standard guide to parliamentary procedure. *The A-B-C's of Parliamentary Procedure* is a simplified version of the information provided in *Robert's Rules of Order*.

The Nature of Minutes

As their name implies, minutes should be brief. Brevity, however, often requires more effort and thought than long-windedness.

It is not necessary for the secretary to be a member of the board. Often, boards hire a professional secretary, an assistant secretary or a clerk to take the minutes. If the secretary is a director, hiring a minute recorder enables the board secretary to participate in the debate. At a minimum, meeting minutes should contain the following elements:

Type of meeting. Meetings are usually described in minutes as regular, special, adjourned regular or adjourned special meetings.

Association name. Record the association's corporate name and the words "Minutes of the meeting of (name of body)."

Event information. Specify the meeting date, time and location.

Attendants' names. List the names of directors or members present, the name of the presiding officer, and secretary or substitute minute recorder. For open meetings, the nonvoting audience need not be included. However, if the meeting is a membership meeting, a roll should be taken, and the number of persons or votes present—or at least a quorum—should be announced and entered into the minutes. The roll can be taken at the door by using a check list.

Approval of the previous minutes. Unless the assembly waives the reading of the minutes, they should be read and approved or corrected. If corrections are necessary, the board should approve the minutes as corrected. Previous meeting minutes are not approved at a special meeting—the minutes should be approved at the next regular meeting. If regular meetings are held less than quarterly, a special committee or the executive committee can be appointed to approve the minutes.

Officer and committee reports. Reports made by the manager, board, and committee members often precede the business of the meeting. Such reports are usually for information only, and if in writing, can be appended to the minutes with board approval. If not in writing, only the fact that the report was made needs to be stated in the minutes. If they contain recommendations for board action, motions to adopt or implement these recommendations should be made by a member other than the reporting officer and acted upon by the board. The board's disposal of the motion may appear in the minutes.

The business of the meeting. The minutes should follow the agenda, unless the assembly agrees to take a matter out of order. The resolutions, exactly as finally made, seconded, and passed, should be grouped according to subject matter. There is no reason to include the summary of debates, discussions, drafts, and revisions of the motions. None of this constitutes official action of the assembly. The resolution appearing in the minutes should be as voted upon and passed. If there are reports, they should be accepted by resolution without adoption of recommendations and appended to the minutes. The minutes should show each motion as voted upon and how it was disposed, passed, defeated, tabled, returned to committee, etc. In addition, the minutes should include points of order, appeals—whether sustained or lost—and the chair's reason for the ruling.

The resolution should contain a description—including a background statement and introduction—of the matter before the assembly for discussion and approval. The assembly will vote on the language of the background statement and resolution. Again, the remarks of individual members should not be included in the minutes. Members' remarks do not constitute actions of the assembly, and can lead to future misinterpretations of the assembly's actions.

In a well-run meeting, the text of the motion will be presented in writing before it is brought to action. If it is included on the meeting agenda, appears in the conclusion of a committee report, or is presented as a written recommendation by the manager, it is more likely that the assembly will make a sound decision based on revisions and narrowly discussed amendments.

In light of the above reasoning, the motion should be made before the topic is discussed. No motion, no discussion. A discussion without a motion is not only officially "out of order," but also creates chaos. A committee report can be made, ending in a motion, if action is required. If no action is required, there must still be a motion to accept the report without action.

Minutes must reflect correct parliamentary procedure. The assembly should not discuss anything that is not properly "on the floor," meaning presented in the form of a motion that the assembly can act upon, or a request for a ruling that the chair can act upon.

The only exception to this rule may be a guest speaker. Because the assembly only recognized the speaker, his or her speech is not the action of the assembly. In such an instance, only the speaker's name and general topic of the speech should be indicated in the minutes, unless the assembly moves that the speech be attached to the minutes.

The worst examples of minute taking contain extraneous material. Taking minutes is not equivalent to taking dictation. The secretary's notes should be used as a reference to ensure that motions are worded exactly as passed. If the secretary, or any member is uncertain about the wording of a motion, it should be reread before final passage.

In a fast-moving meeting, it may be worthwhile to tape the assembly's actions to ensure that the secretary accurately records the motions. Tape recordings and secretary notes are not official records of the assembly's actions. Therefore, neither should be available for inspection or be included in association records. I recommend boards destroy meeting tapes and notes when the minutes are adopted.

A motion is the agreed upon solution to a problem. The actual direction for action by a board should begin with the word "resolved." A motion passed by the board is properly described as a "resolution." The resolution of the problem may have been stated in the background statement and discussed during the debate.

The vote. If the vote is "without objection"—the fastest method of passing routine motions—it should be so stated in the minutes. If the vote is by voice, only the chair's ruling needs to be noted by stating "the motion passed." If a member successfully moves to divide the assembly by standing, a show of hands, or a paper ballot, the count should be recorded. For small assemblies, such as association boards or committees, it is proper to show the names of those abstaining, and voting in favor of and in opposition to resolutions and motions. It is especially important to list those dissenting. This way, if they disagree with the board's actions, they are not held responsible for the consequences.

Adjournment. The last paragraph should state the time of adjournment.

Secretary's signature. The signature of the secretary, preceded by the word "submitted," must be included at the end of the minutes.

Approval at a subsequent meeting. The minutes are not official until they are approved by the assembly at a subsequent meeting. However, if the subsequent meeting is too far in the future, a committee should be appointed to approve the minutes. Once approved, they are the official action of the assembly, regardless of what actually occurred. Thus, by approving the minutes with a differing statement of a resolution, an assembly can effectively change a passed motion. Minutes can be corrected even after they are approved by a "Motion to Amend a (passed) Motion Previously Adopted," which requires a two-thirds vote, a majority vote with notice, or a majority of the entire membership if that is more practical. Minutes cannot be changed to reconsider something that has already occurred, such as issuing a payment or signing a contract agreement.

Inclusion in the corporate record book. The secretary's primary responsibility is maintaining the association's official records. The minute book is the association's principal record. The records should be printed on quality paper, in an official notebook. The notebook should be turned over to the succeeding secretary upon appointment or election to office.

Publication. While publishing minutes is generally not required, it is recommended. Minutes should be available for examination by any member upon request.

Board and membership meeting minutes are the sole, official reflection of the association's actions. Without them, an association has not acted. Minutes that reflect members' remarks and not the assembly's actions are useless. By including the proper elements in meeting minutes and following parliamentary procedure, association boards and officers can conduct business in an effective and productive manner. ❧

> *Gurdon Buck is a founder and director of CAI's Connecticut Chapter. He is a former member of CAI's Board of Trustees and a past president of CAI's Research Foundation. Buck has written several books, articles and newspaper columns about community associations. He is a community association attorney and urban planner in Hartford, Connecticut and the recipient of the 1987 Byron Hanke Award.*

Sample Board Meeting Minutes

By Gurdon Buck

Stonemason Village Condominium Association, Inc.
Minutes of the Meeting of the Executive Board

The regular monthly meeting of the executive board of Stonemason Village Condominium Association, Inc. was held on Tuesday, January 19, 1999 at 8:30 p.m. at the clubhouse. The president chaired the meeting and the secretary was present. All members of the board were present. Mr. Hugh L. Dewey, counsel to the association, and Mr. John Handyperson, association manager, were also present.

The minutes of the last meeting were read and approved as corrected.

The treasurer reported the receipt of an unbudgeted bill from the Acme View Plumbing Company for the water leak on December 15 in the amount of $975.00. It was:

RESOLVED: That the bill from the Acme Plumbing Company be paid.

Following debate, it was:

RESOLVED: That the contract with the vending machine company for the candy machine in the clubhouse lobby be continued and the president is authorized to execute the contract. A copy of the contract is to be appended to the minutes.

The social committee report was received and placed on file without objection.

The report of a special committee to investigate and report on additional handicapped parking facilities near the clubhouse was presented by its chair, Ms. Smith. After debate and amendments, a resolution was adopted as follows:

BACKGROUND: The building official of the Town of Saltonstall, following a complaint from Mrs. Jones of Unit 2B, who has a handicapped son visiting her, checked the parking layout of that cluster and pointed out that the Fair Housing Act and state law require the installation of three additional handicapped parking spaces in that lot, reasonably convenient to the main entrance of the building. The manager submitted a sketch plan showing the conversion of five regular spaces to handicapped spaces at the entrance, and the construction of three new spaces at the south end of the parking lot.

RESOLVED: That the manager contract for the construction of the three additional spaces and the striping and signage of handicapped parking spaces in accordance with the standards for such spaces required by the Town of Saltonstall and the sketch plan. The manager should obtain three bids for the work, and submit the lowest responsible bidder's construction contract to the board for approval at the next meeting.

The resolution relating to the use of the game room by nonmembers for parties that was postponed from the last meeting was then taken up. The chair then announced that the guest speaker invited to speak to the board, Mr. Hugh L. Dewey, counsel to the association, would require an earlier departure and should be taken out of order.

Without objection, the motion and pending amendment were laid on the table.

Without objection, the agenda was modified to ask the guest speaker to speak out of order.

The president then introduced Mr. Hugh L. Dewey, who spoke about assessment collection and rule enforcement.

Without objection, the resolution relating to the use of the game room by nonmembers was taken from the table. After amendment and further debate, the motion was made as follows:

RESOLVED: That the manager would prepare and present to the board at its next meeting a draft contract for the rental of the game room to nonmembers for parties and functions. The manager would present a schedule of charges and extra services that would be provided. The association accountant would be asked to comment and advise the association on the accounting for the income.

Mr. Gordon asked for a division of the board by a show of hands. The motion passed by a vote of 5 to 2.

Upon motion made by Mr. Gordon it was:

RESOLVED: That the association undertake the establishment of a summer program for teenagers on its lakefront property. Ms. Thomas moved to amend the motion by inserting the words "preteens and" before "teenagers." The amendment passed. The motion to establish the program, with the pending amendment, was referred to a committee of three to be appointed by the chair with instructions to report program details at the next meeting. The chair appointed Mr. Gordon, Mr. Dorsey and Ms. Thomas to the committee.

The meeting adjourned at 10:05 p.m.

[signature line here]

Marge Scrivener, Secretary

by Richard Lievens

Minutes and Resolutions: The Legal Perspective | ACCURATE RECORDS PROVE BOARD AUTHORITY

TOO OFTEN, community managers and directors regard board meeting minutes and resolutions as ministerial rather than integral to an association's operation and longevity. These duties must never be taken lightly.

Recording Corporate Acts
The basic purpose of maintaining a minute book is to have a record of corporate acts, or board actions. Under appropriate circumstances,

these records will prove invaluable in upholding a corporate act, proving authority, rebutting a presumption of authority, or defending directors.

When someone attacks or challenges the validity of a given corporate act, properly kept minutes and resolutions will help verify the board's authority to make such a decision. Clearly, minutes or resolutions do not create authority where there is none. The applicable statutes, the articles of incorporation, or association bylaws must create the authority; the minutes and resolutions prove the authority as it was exercised. If no authority exists, no such authority can be exercised.

Minutes and resolutions can also be used to rebut the presumption of authority. For example, the president of a corporation presumably has the authority to perform certain acts. Through proper resolutions recorded in the minutes, other board members may deny such authority—and thus are able to prove, if necessary, that no such authority existed on the president's behalf.

Directors should take great care in ensuring that minutes and resolutions properly reflect voting, abstentions and objections. This documentation will protect them if a claim of a breach of fiduciary duty is made against them. The minutes can also reflect an individual director's intentions, acts and omissions, through evidence of voting or dissent. Therefore, it is important for a disagreeing board member to ensure that his or her dissention is properly recorded in the minutes.

When a board takes an action outside the regular course of business, there should be a memorandum or record in the minutes. This record reflects the board's decision to take the action or refusal to take the action. Again, the purpose is to provide evidence of corporate authority and to defend the board if its action is challenged.

While certain actions, such as decisions to sue, should always be recorded in the minutes, actions that are covered by routine, previously approved guidelines, such as assessment collection procedures, need not be so specifically stated in the minutes.

It is worth emphasizing that recording a corporate act in the minutes will not validate the act if the board had no such authority. Likewise, failing to record a valid act in the minutes will not necessary render the act invalid. For example, a resolution duly voted upon and properly reflected in the minutes for an association to purchase real estate does not make the purchase valid if the board lacked such authority. Conversely, if a board exercises its authority to purchase real estate, but through error or omission fails to record the action in the minutes, the corporate act is not necessarily void. It is, however, voidable if the events of the meeting cannot be substantiated in any other way.[1]

Statutory Foundation

Most state laws governing corporations contain specific provisions regarding the taking of minutes. Corporations are subject to the applicable Business Corporation Act or Non-Profit Corporation Act of the controlling jurisdiction. Most such laws require corporations to keep minutes of shareholder and director meeting proceedings.[2] Therefore, association boards should analyze applicable statutes to determine minimum minute-taking requirements.

Failure to keep contemporaneous minutes as mandated by statute will not necessarily void the corporate act. For example, if the minutes are amended after the fact, this may be sufficient to satisfy statutory requirements.[3] However, if an association refused to repay a loan based on the argument that the promissory note was unenforceable—because authorization to obtain the loan was not recorded in the minutes—such an argument would probably fail. A court would likely find that regardless of the statutory obligation to take minutes, if the association received the benefit of the loan it could not defeat the creditor's claim by merely showing that the transaction was not recorded in the minutes.[4]

In addition to the minimum statutory requirements to keep minutes, the Rules of Evidence (for use in litigation) in most jurisdictions provide that a corporation's records must only be attested by the president and secretary's signature. These documents, accompanied with a corporate seal or certificate, constitute competent evidence in any action or proceeding in which the corporation is involved. Evidence statutes provide associations with an invaluable advantage. When an association is involved in a lawsuit, its minutes or resolutions may, under proper circumstances, be introduced into evidence. Generally, it would not be necessary for witnesses to testify about what happened at the meeting or event.

Under limited circumstances, the court may prohibit witnesses from presenting testimony that would impeach or contradict the minutes.[5] Furthermore, excerpts from corporation minutes, which are maintained according to applicable law and identified by the corporation secretary who recorded the minutes and maintained the minute book, can be admissible as evidence in most jurisdictions. Some courts have emphasized that minutes of a corporation board meeting are *prima facie* evidence of the facts.[6] The minutes will speak for themselves without the need for witnesses or other evidence to prove the acts. This is particularly advantageous for associations if an excessive amount of time has elapsed between the board meeting and court proceeding.

The statutory application of minute taking imposed on profit and nonprofit corporations is the same. Case law decisions from jurisdictions nationwide, however, have differentiated these minute-taking standards from those of closely held corporations—corporations that offer no shares for sale and are owned by only a few shareholders who actively conduct the business. Under proper circumstances, the closely held association directors' actions need not be proven by the minutes,[7] but can be proven by oral testimony.[8]

Drafting Meeting Minutes

Minutes should always be drafted during the meeting and approved by the board within a reasonable time. Occasionally, however, minutes are neither drafted nor approved until weeks or months after the meeting. Although this is not an advisable practice, at least one court has held that this action is acceptable, noting that subsequent approval of director meeting minutes is a common practice in corporate offices.[9]

Other courts have extended this concept further but have warned against fabricating minutes.[10] If the minutes are incorrect, courts will probably be liberal in allowing boards to correct them in accordance with the truth.[11]

Minutes and resolutions serve definite legal purposes. Meeting minutes protect board members, uphold and defend corporate acts, prove authority and serve as evidence in court cases. Community associations, typically organized as nonprofit corporations, are subject to minute-taking statutes and requirements. Properly executed minutes and resolutions benefit every corporate entity. Minute-taking statutes and requirements serve a protective—not a burdensome—purpose. ❧

> *Richard Lievens is a partner with Frank, Elmore, Lievens, Chesney & Turet, L.L.P. in Houston. Lievens is a former member of the State Bar of Texas Condominium and Cooperative Housing Committee, a past president of CAI's Greater Houston Area Chapter, and a former adjunct instructor of real estate law, contracts, and community association law at the University of Houston Real Estate Institute.*

References

1. *Cameron and Willacy Counties Community Projects, Inc. et al v. Gonzales*, 614 S.W.2d 585 (Tex. Civ. App. Corpus Christi, reh. den. 1981)

2. *Cameron*, Id.

3. *Cameron*, Id.

4. *Scott v. Potter Plumbing* 596 S.W.2d 492 (MO Ct. App. So. Dist. 1980)

5. *Emergency Patient Services, Inc. v. Crisp*, 602 S.W.2d 26 (MO. Ct. App. Western Dist. 1980)

6. *Acmer v. State Transport*, 549 P.2d 1114 no writ

7. *Kann v. Keystone Resources, Inc.*, 575 F. Supp. 1084 (1983)

8. In re *Eastern Erectors, Inc.* 346 F. Supp. 293

9. *Whitley v. Pacific Industries, Inc.*, 239 N.E.2d 207

10. *National Surety Corporation v. Crystal Springs Fishing Village*, 326 F. Supp. 1171 (1971)

11. *Hallindale v. State*, 326 So.2d 202

CHAPTER 4

Recording Meetings

by Raymond Diaz and
Lucia Anna Trigiani

Boards, Meetings, and Videotape

WHAT YOU NEED TO
KNOW BEFORE YOU TURN
ON THE CAMERA

EVERY COMMUNITY ASSOCIATION needs accurate, permanent minutes. One way to accomplish this is by taping meetings. Taping can create a complete, vivid, and lasting record of not just decisions, but of the discussions that lead to decisions. But is taping a meeting a good idea?

A condominium in Virginia doesn't think so.

In 1993, a unit owner filed a lawsuit asking the court to prevent her association from erasing audiotapes of board meetings. She also asked for permission to videotape meetings. (See sidebar, page 53). In response, the board of directors explained that it used the audiotapes to help prepare formal, written minutes. Once the minutes are approved, the audiotapes are reused—another meeting is taped over the earlier meeting. Until the audiotape is reused, owners can review it. This, the board asserted, was a reasonable policy it had the right to make.

The board also claimed it had the discretion to decide how its meetings would be conducted. Since board members felt videotaping would be disruptive and impede free discussion, they voted not to allow videotaping. The court, the board argued, should not interfere since the association documents placed the decision within the board's discretion.

The owner used Virginia condominium law and the U.S. Constitution to support her request for court assistance. But the court agreed with the association. It found that the law allowed the board to adopt a reasonable record retention policy and to run its meetings as it chose, as long as it met statutory requirements.

As this case shows, taping can be troubling because it involves important, competing considerations. On one hand, owners should have access to as much information as possible about the business of their association. Meeting tapes are an excellent way for owners to review why and how decisions were made. On the other hand, verbatim records can be used to harm an association and, indirectly, the owners' investment.

There are good reasons both for keeping and not keeping audiotapes or videotapes with an association's permanent records. Community associations should consider these benefits and drawbacks before deciding their own policy. It is not an easy decision. Each association's policy depends on where it strikes the balance between these considerations.

You Oughta Be In Pictures

Perhaps the most obvious reason to tape a meeting is the need for accurate minutes. Like any business, an association needs the formal record of its actions and decisions to be accurate. Statutes confirming the right of owners, contract purchasers, and others to review association records have added force to the need for good records and, therefore, accurate minute taking. If the meeting is taped, minute takers can compare the tape to their notes to double-check accuracy.

Taping makes minute taking more convenient. It allows the minute taker to transcribe the minutes without rushing to complete them before they forget the details of decisions. Written notes sometimes fail to refresh the memory. Recording meetings on tape also allows the secretary to participate more fully in the meeting. Because the meeting is taped, the minute taker, who may often be a voting member of the board, is better able to participate in discussions, freed from the preoccupation that complete note-taking requires. Cryptic notes can be fleshed out later by reviewing the meeting tape.

For some associations, tape recordings may also save money. Many communities employ minute takers or pay staff members to attend meetings and take minutes. These meeting costs can be-

Should Boards Tape Meetings?

What are the pros?
- Members can review how decisions were made
- Tapes help create accurate minutes
- Minute takers can transcribe minutes without rushing
- Minute takers can participate in discussions
- Associations don't need paid staff to take minutes

What are the cons?
- Tapes can be used as ammunition by opponents
- More business may be conducted in private, away from tapes
- Directors may be hesitant to speak when being taped
- Others may "grandstand," adding to meeting time
- Tapes are not always reliable—information may be lost

come a significant budget line item. If the meeting is recorded, the tape may be transcribed and developed into minutes by a staff person or other minute taker who is not paid for attending the meeting.

Taping benefits the members, too. It allows members who did not attend a meeting to witness the discussion and decision-making process that occurred. Written minutes create a formal record, but they don't convey the full meeting deliberations, replete with inflections and asides. Tapes do.

Lights, Camera—Lawsuit?

Taping meetings can cause problems, however. When meeting tapes are used as evidence, they are frequently introduced *against* an association. While this is not reason enough to not tape meetings, it is reason to review the arguments against preserving tapes.

An association speaks by its formal resolutions. These resolutions should be complete enough to explain what action is being taken, what authority is relied on to take it, and why the action is taken. Tapes of discussions that led to formal resolutions can serve as ammunition for those who later cast doubt on the motivation or intent of a resolution. It can allow opponents to "rewrite history."

Taping meetings may also result in more business being conducted in executive session. Most statutes allow boards of directors to convene in closed session for a number of specific purposes. Frequently, in an effort to allow owners as much information as possible, boards will take up matters in open session.

If the board becomes concerned that a verbatim record of their discussions may become available to third parties, they may feel obliged to move into closed session. The board may think that it is better to discuss matters in private than to make those discussions available to someone who may use them against the association.

Another common criticism of taping minutes is that it can restrict discussion and stifle free exchange among the meeting participants. Most associations and their boards can make decisions only in a meeting, unless everyone consents in writing. Discussion, debate, and the free exchange of points of view will frequently lead to the best decision. Many board members, however, are hesitant to speak openly when they are being taped. They become self-conscious or fear that their words may come back to haunt them or their association. Free discussion leads to better decisions. Taping may put that in jeopardy.

In the Virginia lawsuit mentioned on page 44, one director testified that she was unwilling to mention another association's bad experience with a company during an open meeting—a company the board was about to contract. The reason? She knew the meeting was being taped. Another director testified that he was intimidated by the video camera an owner was running during the meeting. He was afraid that whatever he said might "show up on the six o'clock news."

Not everyone is intimidated by a camera. Taping meetings may cause some participants to "grandstand." Some people light up when they see the red light on a camera or tape recorder. Brevity goes out the window, histrionics becomes the order of the day, and meetings end in the wee hours of the morning. Often, the only means of ensuring brief, business-like meetings is to turn the machines off.

The Camera Never Blinks

In this visual, electronic age, it's easy to see how helpful meeting tapes can be. But they can also cause problems. Consider the following examples:

- One association videotaped its meetings for later broadcast on closed circuit television. During a debate on a particularly contentious issue, charges, counter-charges, and epithets were hurled between homeowners and directors. As tempers cooled, apologies were extended. Yet months later, a director, having failed in a reelection bid, filed a slander claim against the association and several of its directors. Exhibit number one? The videotape preserved in the association's records.

- Another board kept audiotapes of its meetings. At one meeting it resolved to accept a vendor's contract on certain conditions. The decision and conditions were part of the written minutes approved by the board. The audiotape of the meeting, though never approved by the board or made an "official" record, was retained. When a dispute arose after the contract was signed, the vendor used the taped debate to successfully argue that it was never supposed to perform one of the conditions in the written resolution.

The reliability of tapes, especially audiotapes, can also be a problem. Occasionally, important statements are not picked up by the taping machine. Sometimes a tape runs out or breaks unnoticed. If tapes are used as a substitute for written minutes or to augment bare-bones notes, an association may find itself with no record of its actions.

Considerations If You Tape

Each community must reach its own conclusion on whether to tape its meetings. If it does tape, it must decide how long meeting tapes will be kept as part of the association's records. Both of these questions require a review of the pros and cons described in this article.

Once a policy is established, owners must be aware of it and understand the reasons it was adopted. If the decision is made to tape meetings, that decision is incomplete unless the board also establishes a records management plan. The records management plan should address what meetings will be taped, who may tape, the availability of tapes for review and copying, and how long the tapes will be maintained.

An important element of the records management plan should be a clear procedure dealing with closed or executive sessions and with minutes of those sessions. There is no reason for closed sessions to be taped. Most states allow a board to only discuss matters in closed session and require formal action to be taken in open session. Owners can't participate in closed sessions. Thus, even if an association elects to tape its open meetings, it should think long and hard before creating a tape of executive sessions that may, one day, become available to an opponent of the association.

Like good government, the effective conduct of a community association's affairs are a series of compromises among important, competing considerations. Successfully striking balances as each compromise is considered is the mark of a successful community. Whether or not to tape association meetings is another issue on which a reflective board must exercise leadership and judgment. The decision that is made should be based on the best interests of the association—not to circumvent owners' rights to information. Any taping should be governed by reasonable restrictions intended to protect association confidences. ❧

Raymond Diaz is a shareholder in the Vienna, Virginia law firm of Rees, Broome & Diaz, P.C. Lucia Anna Trigiani is an attorney with Mays & Valentine, L.L.P. in McLean, Virginia.

by Henry Goodman

Tape Recording
Meetings

DECIDING WHETHER TAPING
MEETINGS IS PRACTICAL
FOR YOUR COMMUNITY

WHEN A DISSIDENT GROUP of owners in a Massachusetts condominium claimed the board meeting minutes did not accurately reflect their views, the board of directors announced it would begin taping meetings. The goal was to create more accurate minutes. But the dissidents then alleged it was illegal to tape their comments without their permission, and that doing so showed a lack of respect. They refused to grant permission. The board, although it believed that taping was legal, destroyed the tape out of respect for the dissidents.

As the association's attorney, it seemed strange to me that the board showed such respect for a group that planned to unseat it. A group so concerned that its arguments lacked substance that it did not want its words preserved on tape. Nonetheless, this case raises legitimate issues about recording. Can comments at a meeting be legally taped and used when a speaker states that he or she objects to the taping, and refuses to allow the board to press "record?"

In some states, privacy and wiretapping laws grant every individual the right to prevent his or her conversations or messages from being recorded or intercepted. In fact, such laws make such interception (including tape recording) a crime. In these statutes the term "interception" means to secretly hear, secretly record—or aid another in doing so—the contents of any wire or oral communication. The key word is "secretly." If the board announces at the beginning of the meeting—and every time a person enters—that the meeting is being recorded, the recording is not a secret. Therefore, the board can legally tape record the meeting if it follows that formula. Thus, it is legal to record the minutes of a meeting, despite objections, so long as the recording is not a secret. Secret recordings can be a crime with severe penalties. In Massachusetts, for example, secret taping is considered illegal wiretapping.

In some state statutes, taping is illegal only if the spoken word is in a private forum, not a public forum. An open board meeting would likely constitute an public forum.

Those Who Object

Community association attorneys often disagree about the benefits of taping. In my opinion, taping is desirable.

Taping helps the secretary or clerk prepare the written minutes accurately. Although it is not necessary to quote each speaker verbatim, it allows the secretary to quote important phraseology. If disputes erupt, the association can save recordings to determine what was actually said at the meeting.

What about the people who object? They still have a right to not be recorded. They can leave the meeting or remain and not speak. If they do speak, their words may be recorded and, if applicable, used against them. Their mere objection is insufficient.

On occasion someone with something important to say will refuse to say it into a tape recorder. There's a danger in permitting unrecorded communication—the individual may later deny actually making such statements, rendering it worthless.

Nonetheless, the board may occasionally need to hear such comments. But what if the speaker is intimidated? Sometimes speakers want nothing that proves they're making accusations against another owner. They may not want to be on tape suggesting something unpopular. Yet the board may consider such information to be crucial. In an appropriate situation, the board could vote to suspend taping. However, the minutes should still show that the board responded to the information imparted by the speaker. In my opinion, the minutes should reflect more than the board's ultimate decision. It should show the information upon which the board based its actions.

Are there options available when residents refuse to be taped or to have a record made of their comments? Of course. In my opinion, however, this is weak information. For example, a person may secretly give information to a board member who is supposed to impart it to the board. The board member may be sworn to secrecy as to the speaker's identity. But the alleged facts would amount to hearsay. If there is a conflict, the board cannot rely on such unsubstantiated third-hand information in court.

Members Taping Meetings

Sometimes homeowners either openly or secretly tape board meetings without the board's permission. And once directors learn a homeowner is recording their discussions and decisions, they usually question whether they must allow the taping to continue.

I would argue that the board's statements and actions during an open meeting are public in nature and, therefore, are not susceptible to privacy protections.

When the board has a legitimate interest in keeping its actions private, it may retire to executive session. (*See Chapter 5*). Issues that a board may discuss during executive session include:

- Potentially defamatory matters, such as complaints of criminal activity
- Matters in which an owner may have a right to privacy, such as financial issues
- Privileged matters, such as attorney/client advice or litigation strategy

Meetings held to discuss the above issues are not open to the public. All private conversations are subject to the prohibition of secret taping. If the taping is open and obvious, the board may eject the individual recording the meeting.

A Double-edged Sword

Some lawyers disagree with taping entirely. One of my partners, Seth Emmer, a member of CAI's Board of Trustees, believes that taping meeting minutes is a bad idea. He feels that minutes should memorialize decisions—not what was said. However, he agrees that divergent votes should be recorded. Seth also believes record-

Board Has Power to Bar
Videotaping of Meetings

By Raymond Diaz

IN *OLSON* v. *ROTONDA* Condominium Unit Owners Association (Chancery No. 121441, Circuit Court of Fairfax County, Virginia, 1993), Constance Olson, a unit owner at the Rotonda Condominium, sued the condominium association seeking a determination that a policy resolution adopted by the board of directors was unlawful. The resolution barred videotaping of board meetings and provided that audiotapes were to be erased after the board approved the minutes.

When several owners became dissatisfied with the association's management by the board of directors, they attempted to videotape an open meeting of the board. In reaction, the board adopted a resolution that barred videotaping board meetings. Going further, the board formalized an existing practice by also resolving that audiotapes of board meetings made by the professional secretary were to be erased once written minutes of each taped meeting were approved.

During the 30 to 60 days between the time the audiotapes were made and the minutes approved, the audiotapes were available to all owners at the association's on-site office.

A temporary restraining order was entered barring the erasure of any audiotape until a full hearing could be held. After the full hearing, the temporary restraining order was dissolved, and the court ordered that the entire case be dismissed with prejudice, thus allowing the board to prohibit videotaping of its meetings and allowing audiotapes to be erased after the written minutes were approved.

In support of her request that the board be prevented from erasing audiotapes, Olson pointed to the provision of the Virginia Condominium Act ("Act") requiring that association records be available for inspection by owners and contract purchasers. She argued that the audiotapes were records of the association and, if erased, would not be available for inspection.

The trial court found that the Act did not preclude the association from adopting a reasonable records retention policy. The court noted that Olson's argument would compel the court to conclude that the Act required a condominium association to maintain every piece of paper or celluloid in its records in perpetuity. The court labeled such a result "a manifest absurdity" and found no basis to inject itself into the business of the association to rewrite its policy.

In seeking an order permitting her to videotape open board meetings, Olson argued that the Act was in derogation of the common law and, therefore, must be strictly construed. Under such a construction, the board had only those powers that the Act granted to it. Since the Act did not expressly authorize the board to prohibit videotaping, it could not do so.

The trial court found this logic to be flawed because it failed to recognize that statutes may empower both by their express provisions and by necessary implication. The Act permits bylaws to delegate powers to boards of directors. Here, there was a very broad grant of authority to the board. That grant was consistent with the Act and was sufficient to allow the board to adopt rules regarding the conduct of meetings.

The court also relied on the fact that the association was incorporated as additional authority for the board's right to prohibit videotaping. Since the Act authorized condominium associations to be incorporated, it recognized that association boards might have the powers that the Virginia Nonstock Corporations Act ("Corporations Act") granted. Therefore, the Rotonda directors were vested with the broad authority granted to boards of directors by the Corporations Act. That statutory grant of power was also sufficient to allow the board of directors to adopt the rule against videotaping.

Finally, the court addressed and disposed of Olson's claim that the board's resolution violated her constitutional rights. It concluded that there was no state action sufficient to implicate the Constitution, and therefore, constitutional scrutiny of the board's rulemaking was not in order.

ing can be stifling. A person with information may be afraid to have his words on tape. Ultimately, says Seth, taping has no practical use and can come back to "bite the board."

In that regard, taping can be a double-edged sword. The tape—and the statements contained on the tape—could be used not only against a speaker, but also against the board. This is especially true if the owner is speaking on behalf of the board or if the board acts wrongly.

This doesn't mean speakers should fear taping. Most minutes simply record the gist of a speaker's comments. Taping is more accurate. A speaker's comments are less likely to be mischaracterized. In fact, the mere knowledge that the tape is rolling may cause board members to think about their positions and make more rational decisions.

Store Tapes for At Least One Year

If the board decides to tape, it should establish a policy on how long to keep tapes before destroying them. Generally, I recommend keeping tapes for at least a year. Tapes containing controversial matters can be kept much longer.

One additional word of advice: do not tape executive sessions where you are discussing personalities, legal strategies, or matters covered by privacy rights. Such information can fall into the wrong hands and the board could be sued. The board could also lose its claim that the issues are privileged information.

Although minutes need not be verbatim transcripts, they should accurately reflect the speaker's position. They should also reflect the board's ultimate decision. If a decision is wrong and the board is sued, dissenters may be saved from liability—they can show they did not go along with the decision. It is also helpful politically, in the next election, to be able to show the voting positions of each of the incumbents running for reelection, as well as the attitude and position of a board member who is being recalled. ❧

Henry Goodman is a principal in the law firm of Marcus, Goodman, Emmer & Brooks, P.C. in Braintree, Massachusetts. He is also admitted to practice law in Florida.

CHAPTER 5

Executive
Sessions

Behind Closed Doors | WHEN IS IT APPROPRIATE FOR BOARDS TO MEET IN EXECUTIVE SESSIONS?

MOST COMMUNITY ASSOCIATIONS REALIZE the importance of holding open board meetings. There are times, however, when a board needs to meet in closed executive sessions.

So when can a board meet behind closed doors? The answer may lie in your state's condominium or homeowner association laws. Some states, such as Florida, require all board meetings to be open. In Virginia, boards are required to vote before entering executive session. Other state statutes specifically list the topics that can be discussed in executive sessions.

In general, most experts consider the following subjects to be appropriate for closed meetings: pending litigation, personnel issues, and contract negotiations.

Pending litigation would include any action taken by the association, from construction defect suits to actions against covenant violators. Personnel issues could include harassment suits and job performance.

"Executive sessions are good for personal issues," said Ellen Hirsch de Haan, a Florida attorney and a member of CAI's Executive Committee. "It could be discussions of employee issues or a conversation with a homeowner regarding collection problems."

The key is that the executive session, if allowed by state law, is a privilege that should not be abused.

Information is Confidential

Most experts believe executive sessions should be announced in advance to members. The manual for CAI's *ABCs—A Basic Course for Association Leaders* states that members should be informed of any agenda items that will be discussed in executive session. By doing so, members are less likely to be offended when asked to leave a meeting.

"The more openly you communicate, the more you can avoid claims that the board is sneaky," de Haan said.

Even though the meeting may be closed, the results should be recorded in the minutes. If appropriate, communicate the results of a closed meeting, but remember: the information discussed is confidential. While the association may publish that the board met in a closed session to discuss an architectural violation, it should not reveal the member's name or the meeting details.

"Executive sessions are generally considered confidential meetings and they should be viewed as such," said Virginia attorney Ken Chadwick. "If a board member discusses something with a friend that should be confidential, that could lead to trouble."

Chadwick worked with an association that nearly lost its directors and officers coverage due to confidential information that was leaked. The board had split into factions. A member of one faction sued the association. It soon became evident that information discussed in executive session was going to the other side.

This was considered a breach of fiduciary duty, which put the association's directors and officers insurance at risk. Since the board was not cooperating with the prosecution of the case, the insurance carrier said it could no longer defend the association. As a result, Chadwick told the directors they could be personally liable if they refused to keep information confidential.

Closed or Secret?

Though executive sessions are sometimes necessary, boards must be careful not to abuse the privilege. Closed meetings should not be used simply because the board wants to discuss an unpopular subject or avoid confrontation.

"It's a tool that needs to be used in certain circumstances, but should not be misused," Chadwick said.

Boards may think of executive sessions as closed meetings, but members may see them as secret meetings. Avoid that perception by limiting the number of executive sessions held, announcing the sessions in advance, and explaining the reasons for the sessions. ❧

RESOURCES

Buck, Gurdon. "A Guide to Taking Perfectly Proper Minutes." *Common Ground* Vol. 3 No. 6 (November/December 1987): 10-11.

Budd, Kenneth. "Conducting Meetings." *Common Ground* Vol. 12 No. 1 (January/February 1996): 14-18.

Budd, Kenneth. "Head Games." *Common Ground* Vol. 12 No. 3 (May/June 1996): 14-18.

Community Associations Institute. "Behind Closed Doors." *Common Ground* Vol. 11 No. 1 (January/February 1995): 35-36.

Community Associations Institute. "Getting Board Members to Show." *Board Briefs* Vol. 3 No. 4 (July/August 1991): 1.

Corbin, Harold. "Leadership: The Role of the Parliamentarian." *Common Ground* Vol. 4 No. 2 (March/April 1988): 11.

Diaz, Raymond. "Board Has Power to Bar Videotaping of Meetings." *Community Association Law Reporter* Vol. 17 No. 6 (June 1994): 7.

Diaz, Raymond and Trigiani, Lucia Anna. "Boards, Meetings, and Videotape." *Common Ground* Vol. 10 No. 2 (March/April 1994): 28-33.

Goodman, Henry. "Taping Meetings." *Common Ground* Vol. 13 No. 5 (September/October 1997): 35-36.

Keatts, MJ. "Proper Preparation Helps Managers Facilitate Effective Board Meetings." *Community Management* Vol. 4 No. 5 (September/October 1996): 1-2.

Lievens, Richard. "Minutes and Resolutions: The Legal Perspective." *Common Ground* Vol. 3 No. 6 (November/December 1987): 7-9.

Philbin, Peter. "Swatting at Gadflies." *Common Ground* Vol. 10 No. 1 (January/February 1994): 23-27.

Washburn, Pam. "Board Packets Help Reduce Meeting Times." *Community Management* Vol. 5 No. 6 (November/December 1997): 1-2.

To purchase *The A-B-Cs of Parliamentary Procedure*, call CAI at (703) 548-8600.

CONTRIBUTORS

Gurdon Buck is a founder and director of CAI's Connecticut Chapter. He is a former member of CAI's Board of Trustees and a past president of CAI's Research Foundation. Buck has written several books, articles and newspaper columns about community associations. He is a community association attorney and urban planner in Hartford, Connecticut and the recipient of the 1987 Byron Hanke Award.

Kenneth Budd is CAI's director of publications and editor of *Common Ground*.

Harold Corbin is a practitioner of parliamentary procedure and a long-time member of the American Institute of Parliamentarians.

Raymond Diaz is a shareholder in the law firm of Rees, Broome & Diaz, P.C. in Vienna, Virginia.

Henry Goodman is a principal in the law firm of Marcus, Goodman, Emmer & Brooks, P.C. in Braintree, Massachusetts. He is also admitted to practice law in Florida.

MJ Keatts is editor of CAI's *Community Management, CEO Insights, Community Living of Florida* and *Community Living of California*.

Richard Lievens is a partner with Frank, Elmore, Lievens, Chesney & Turet, L.L.P. in Houston. Lievens is a former member of the State Bar of Texas Condominium and Cooperative Housing Committee, a past president of CAI's Greater Houston Area Chapter, and is a former adjunct instructor of real estate law, contracts, and community association law at the University of Houston Real Estate Institute.

Peter Philbin is an attorney with Rees, Broome & Diaz, P.C. in Vienna, Virginia.

Lucia Anna Trigiani is an attorney with Mays & Valentine, L.L.P. in McLean, Virginia.

Pam Washburn, CMCA, AMS, is vice president of operations for the Timber Pines Community Association, Inc. in Spring Hill, Florida.

INDEX